Target Audience for the Book

The book targets individuals and businesses interested in or already engaged in international trade and exports. This includes small and medium enterprises (SMEs), entrepreneurs, manufacturers aiming to enter global markets, and professionals in export-oriented industries. Policymakers and students studying international business or trade can also benefit. The content is tailored to support both beginners and experienced exporters with practical strategies, examples, and guidance on government resources.

About the Book and Its Benefits

The book, "Unlocking Global Markets: A Comprehensive Guide to Successful Exporting from India" provides a comprehensive guide to exporting from India, covering the economic, strategic, and operational aspects of the process. It explains the benefits of exports, including economic growth, foreign exchange generation, and technological advancement, while addressing challenges such as regulatory barriers and cultural differences. Readers will find actionable insights into strategies like market research, quality assurance, branding, financial management, and compliance.

For the target audience, the book serves as a valuable tool to gain practical knowledge, avoid common pitfalls, and leverage government initiatives. It empowers businesses to expand globally, optimize operations, and achieve sustained growth in international markets.

Unlocking Global Markets

This book explores the intricacies of exporting, encompassing its definition, significance, and benefits to economies and businesses. It delves into how exports drive economic growth, generate foreign exchange, promote technological advancement, and create employment opportunities across sectors like automotive, textiles, and food industries. The topic also highlights challenges such as regulatory barriers, cultural differences, and logistical complexities. It discusses key strategies for export success, including market research, product quality, branding, financial management, and compliance with legal and regulatory requirements. Finally, it examines the government's role in supporting exporters through policies, incentives, and infrastructure, alongside the vital contribution of Export Promotion Councils (EPCs) in facilitating trade and providing sector-specific guidance.

Export is the sale of goods or services produced in one country to another country. It's a crucial component of international trade, driving economic growth, job creation, and technological advancement. This book discusses the intricacies of export, exploring its definition, importance, benefits, and challenges.

Export plays a vital role in the global economy, driving growth, job creation, and technological advancement. By understanding the importance of export, you can leverage its benefits and overcome its challenges to achieve success in international markets. Governments, too, can play a crucial role in supporting export activities through policies that promote trade liberalization and facilitate access to foreign markets.

At its core, export involves the transfer of goods or services across national borders. This can encompass a wide range of products and services, from tangible items like automobiles and electronics to intangible offerings such as software and consulting services. The motivations for export can vary, including generating revenue, accessing new markets, diversifying risk, and capitalizing on comparative advantages.

Export plays a pivotal role in driving economic growth and development. It offers several key benefits to a nation:

- **Increased GDP**—Exports contribute significantly to a country's Gross Domestic Product (GDP). When goods and services are sold to foreign markets, they generate income that can be reinvested in the domestic economy, creating jobs and stimulating economic activity.

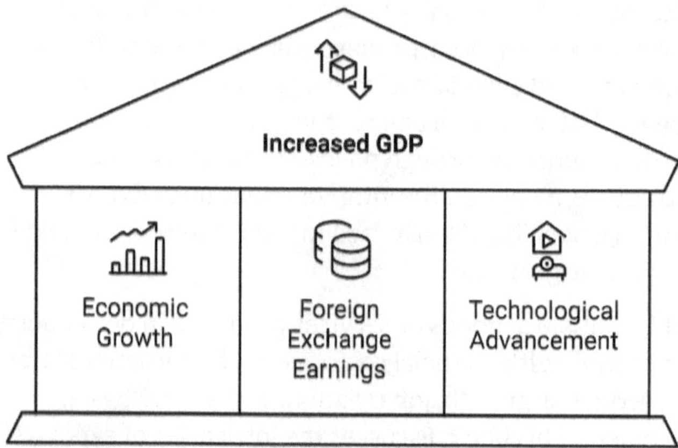

This export-oriented growth leads to:

- <u>Economic Growth</u>—The manufacturing sector including automobile, pharmaceuticals, textiles has contributed substantially to India's GDP, making it one of the fastest-growing economies in the world.

- <u>Foreign Exchange Earnings</u>—Pharmaceuticals, gems and jewelry, textiles and apparel exports are some of the sectors that have brought in significant foreign exchange reserves, strengthening India's economy.

- <u>Technological Advancement</u>—The focus on global markets has driven technological innovation and advancement within the Indian agriculture, healthcare, education industries among others.

- **Job Creation**—Export industries often require a skilled workforce, leading to increased employment opportunities. Moreover, the growth of export-oriented sectors can create indirect jobs in related industries, such as transportation, logistics, and finance. The sector has generated millions of high-skilled jobs, especially in urban areas.

Job Creation through Exports

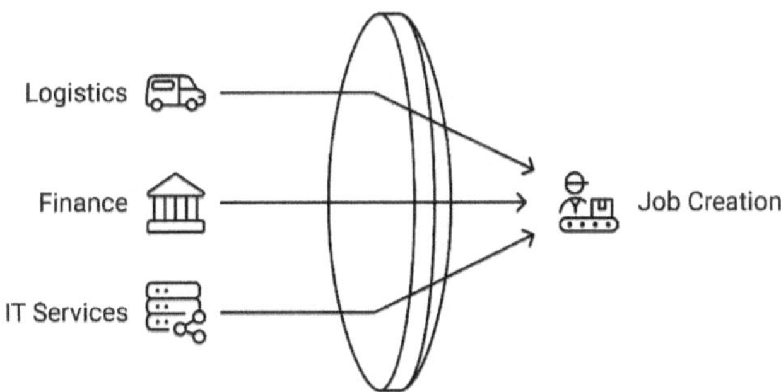

A great example of job creation through exports in the engineering industry is India's automotive sector. As Indian automakers, such as Tata Motors and Mahindra & Mahindra, have increased their global presence, they have expanded their manufacturing facilities and workforce. This growth has not only created direct jobs in manufacturing but also indirect jobs in related sectors like:

- <u>Logistics</u>: Increased demand for efficient transportation of auto parts and finished vehicles has led to the growth of logistics companies.

- <u>Finance</u>: Banks and financial institutions have benefited from the increased lending opportunities to automakers and suppliers.

- <u>IT Services</u>: IT companies have been hired to manage complex supply chain operations and customer relationship management.

In essence, the export-oriented growth of India's automotive industry has had a ripple effect, stimulating job creation across various sectors of the economy.

- **Market Access**—Exporting allows you to tap into larger markets beyond their domestic borders. This can provide opportunities for growth, scale economies, and increased profitability.

Benefits of Market Access

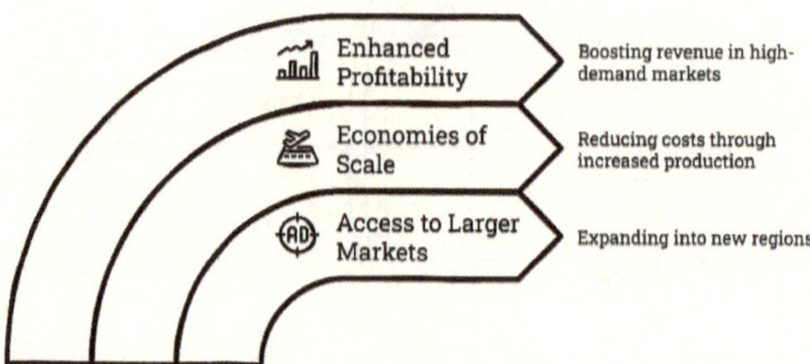

A leading Indian steel manufacturer, Tata Steel, has successfully expanded its operations to the United States. By exporting its high-quality steel products to the US market, Tata Steel has been able to:

- Access a Larger Market: The US market offers significant demand for steel products, particularly in construction and automotive industries.

- Achieve Economies of Scale: Increased production volumes due to exports have allowed Tata Steel to reduce production costs and improve efficiency.

- Enhance Profitability: By selling its products in a high-demand market, Tata Steel has been able to increase its revenue and profitability.

This example demonstrates how exporting can provide significant benefits to engineering companies, including market expansion, cost reduction, and increased revenue.

Another example is Haldiram's. Haldiram's successfully tapped into international markets by exporting its popular products like samosas, namkeens, and sweets. By expanding its reach to countries like the US, UK, and Australia, Haldiram's was able to:

- <u>Increase Market Size</u>: Access a much larger consumer base beyond India, leading to increased sales and revenue.

- <u>Achieve Economies of Scale</u>: Larger production volumes due to increased demand allowed them to optimize production costs.

- <u>Enhance Brand Reputation</u>: International exposure helped strengthen the brand's reputation and recognition.

- <u>Diversify Revenue Streams</u>: Reduced reliance on the domestic market by diversifying into multiple international markets.

By capitalizing on the opportunities offered by exporting, Haldiram's has solidified its position as a global leader in the Indian snack food industry.

- **Diversification**—By selling products and services to multiple countries, exporters can reduce their reliance on any single market. This diversification helps mitigate risks associated with economic fluctuations or political instability in a particular region.

Bharat Forge Ltd., a leading automotive component manufacturer, is a prime example of diversification in Indian exports. Initially focused on the domestic market, the company has successfully expanded its operations to cater to global automotive giants like General Motors, Ford, and Volkswagen. By diversifying its customer base across multiple countries, Bharat Forge has reduced its dependence on any single market, safeguarding its business from economic downturns or geopolitical tensions in specific regions.

- **Technology Transfer**—Exporting can foster technology transfer and innovation. When you compete in global markets, they are often incentivized to develop new products, processes, and technologies to remain competitive.

A prime example of technology transfer in India is the automotive industry. When global automakers like Maruti Suzuki, Hyundai, and Toyota set up manufacturing plants in India, they brought advanced technologies and manufacturing processes. This led to:

- <u>Skill Development</u>: Indian engineers and technicians gained exposure to cutting-edge technologies and best practices.

- <u>Local Innovation</u>: Local suppliers were encouraged to improve their quality standards and production capabilities to meet global standards.

- <u>New Product Development</u>: Indian automakers, like Tata Motors and Mahindra & Mahindra, were able to leverage the technology transfer to develop innovative products, such as electric vehicles and hybrid cars.

- <u>Export Opportunities</u>: The enhanced technological capabilities have enabled Indian automakers to export vehicles to global markets.

This technology transfer has not only boosted the Indian automotive industry but has also contributed to overall economic growth and development.

- **Balance of Payments**—Exports can help improve a country's balance of payments, which is the difference between its exports and imports. A positive balance of payments indicates that a country is generating more foreign exchange through exports than it is spending on imports.

India's textile industry is a prime example of how exports can improve a country's balance of payments. The industry exports a wide range of textile products, including cotton, silk, and synthetic fabrics, to countries around the world.

When Indian textile manufacturers export their products, they earn foreign currency. This foreign currency inflow helps to improve India's balance of payments. By exporting more than it imports in the textile sector, India can strengthen its economic position and reduce its reliance on foreign debt.

Exporting offers numerous advantages to exporters like you, including:

- **Increased Revenue**—Accessing new markets can lead to higher sales volumes and increased revenue.

  The Indian textile industry, a key driver of the country's economy, has greatly benefited from increased exports. By accessing new markets in Europe, the US, Africa and the Middle East, exporters can sell a wider range of products, from cotton fabrics to ready-made garments. This expansion will lead to increased revenue, job creation, and economic growth.

- **Economies of Scale**—Producing larger quantities for export can result in lower production costs per unit.

  The Indian pharmaceutical industry is a global powerhouse, known for producing generic drugs at a fraction of the cost of branded medications. By exporting drugs in large quantities in international markets, pharmaceutical companies can leverage economies of scale.

- **Brand Recognition**—Exporting can enhance a company's brand recognition and reputation in international markets.

  Indian automotive companies like Tata Motors and Mahindra & Mahindra have successfully leveraged exports to enhance their brand recognition globally. By exporting vehicles to countries like South Africa, Australia, and South America, these companies have established a strong brand presence in these regions. This increased brand recognition has not only boosted their sales in international markets but has also positively impacted their domestic sales.

- **Competitive Advantage**—Exporting can provide you with a competitive advantage by allowing them to leverage their unique strengths and capabilities.

  The Indian pharmaceutical industry has gained a significant competitive advantage by exporting generic drugs to global markets. By leveraging its large pool of skilled labour, advanced manufacturing facilities, and rigorous quality control standards, Indian pharmaceutical companies have been able to produce high-quality, low-cost generic drugs. This has enabled them to compete effectively with multinational pharmaceutical companies, capturing a substantial share of the global generic drug market.

Despite its benefits, exporting can also present several challenges:

- **Regulatory Barriers**—Trade regulations, tariffs, and quotas can create obstacles for exporters.

  The Indian automotive industry has faced significant regulatory barriers in many international markets. Tariffs imposed by certain countries on imported vehicles have limited the export potential of Indian car and motorcycle manufacturers. Additionally, stringent emission and safety standards in some countries can be challenging to meet, especially for smaller manufacturers. These regulatory hurdles have hindered the full potential of the Indian automotive industry in the global market.

  Another example is the Indian IT sector, which has faced regulatory challenges in various foreign markets. These challenges often relate to data privacy and security concerns. For instance, some countries have implemented stricter data localization requirements, mandating that specific types of data must be stored within their borders. Such regulatory barriers can hinder the expansion of Indian IT companies into these markets and their ability to provide cloud-based services.

- **Cultural Differences**—Understanding and adapting to different cultural norms and business practices can be challenging.

  Indian companies often face cultural differences when working with clients from Western countries. For instance, direct communication styles, which are common in Western cultures, can sometimes be perceived as rude or aggressive in more indirect cultures.

  Understanding these cultural nuances is essential for effective collaboration and building strong client relationships.

Additionally, differences in work ethics, time management, and decision-making processes can also pose challenges for Indian professionals working in global teams.

Another example is the Indian textile industry. When exporting to Middle Eastern markets, exporters often encounter cultural differences in business practices. For instance, in some Middle Eastern countries, building strong personal relationships is crucial before conducting business. Additionally, understanding local customs and preferences in terms of design, colour, and fabric choices is essential to cater to the specific needs of these markets. Failure to adapt to these cultural nuances can hinder export efforts and lead to missed opportunities.

- **Language Barriers**—Effective communication can be hindered by language differences.

The Indian food industry has experienced significant growth in recent years, with many companies aiming to expand their global footprint. However, language barriers can pose challenges when exporting food products. For example, understanding and complying with food labelling regulations in different countries can be difficult due to varying language requirements and cultural sensitivities. Additionally, effective communication with international buyers and suppliers may be hindered by language differences, which can lead to misunderstandings and delays.

- **Logistics and Transportation**—Coordinating the shipment of goods across borders can be complex and costly.

The Indian automotive industry, a significant exporter of vehicles, faces numerous logistical challenges when shipping cars and components to international markets. These challenges include port congestion, customs delays, and high transportation costs. For instance, shipping a car from India to the US involves multiple modes of transport, including road, rail, and sea. Each mode has its own set of complexities, such as navigating different regulatory frameworks and ensuring timely delivery.

- **Currency Fluctuations**—Exchange rate fluctuations can impact the profitability of exports.

The Indian textile industry is heavily reliant on the import of raw materials like cotton and synthetic fibres. When the Indian rupee depreciates against the US dollar, the cost of these imported raw materials increases. This can erode the profitability of textile exporters, as they may not be able to pass on the increased costs to their customers in foreign markets due to intense competition.

The Indian engineering sector, which exports a wide range of products, from automotive components to heavy machinery, is significantly affected by currency fluctuations. A depreciation of the Indian Rupee can make Indian exports more competitive in international markets, leading to increased demand. However, a sudden appreciation of the Rupee can erode the profitability of these exports, as the value of export earnings in Rupee terms diminishes.

What Strategies Should an Indian Exporter Adopt to Achieve Export Success

There is no single, straightforward formula for export success. A strategy that proves effective for one product may not be suitable for another. Moreover, a strategy that thrives in the US market might falter in Southeast Asia. This underscores the importance of adaptability and flexibility for exporters, who must be prepared to tailor their approach to suit diverse market needs and geographic nuances.

While there's no one-size-fits-all solution, there are fundamental principles that every exporter should grasp and implement to achieve success. These principles, when applied judiciously, can significantly enhance the prospects of international trade.

Firstly, a deep understanding of the target market is paramount. This involves meticulous research into consumer preferences, cultural nuances, and economic conditions. Exporters must identify potential buyers, analyse their needs, and tailor their products or services to meet these specific requirements. Building strong relationships with local distributors and agents can also be instrumental in navigating the complexities of foreign markets.

Secondly, robust product quality and consistent delivery are essential. Exporters must maintain stringent quality control standards and ensure timely delivery to build a strong reputation and customer loyalty. Investing in quality assurance processes and efficient supply chain management can significantly contribute to these goals.

Thirdly, effective marketing and branding are crucial for attracting customers and differentiating oneself from competitors. A well-crafted marketing strategy, incorporating digital marketing, social media, and traditional advertising, can help generate brand awareness and drive sales.

Fourthly, understanding and complying with international trade regulations is imperative. Exporters must familiarize themselves with customs procedures, import duties, and export controls. Engaging with customs brokers and trade consultants can help navigate these complexities and ensure smooth clearance of goods.

Finally, financial management is a critical aspect of export success. Exporters must carefully manage cash flow, mitigate currency exchange risks, and secure adequate financing for their operations. Establishing strong relationships with banks and financial institutions can provide access to essential credit facilities and trade finance solutions.

By mastering these fundamental principles and adapting to the ever-changing dynamics of international trade, exporters can position themselves for long-term success in the global marketplace.

How Every Indian Can Contribute to India's Export Success

India, a nation renowned for its diverse talents and entrepreneurial spirit, possesses the potential to emerge as a global export powerhouse. While large corporations and established exporters play a significant role, individual Indians, ranging from artisans to engineering professionals and from working professionals to retired individuals, can become exporters by establishing their own export businesses. They can achieve this through various avenues:

- **Manufacturing**: you can set up manufacturing units to produce goods for export.

- **Trading**: By identifying high-demand products in overseas markets, you can source these products and export them under their own brand.

- **Export Partnerships**: Collaborating with manufacturers as an export partner can help you leverage their skills and networks to facilitate exports.

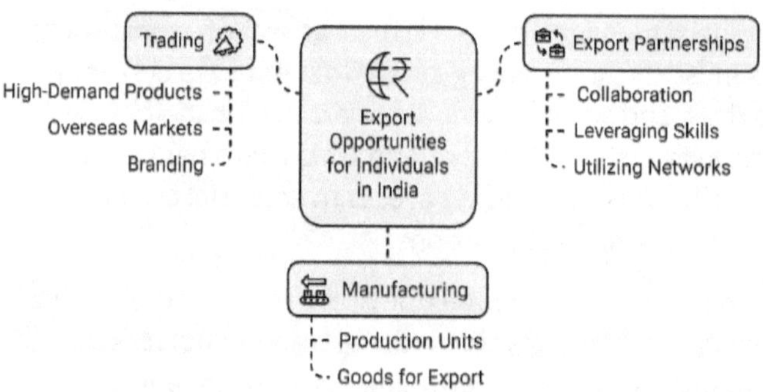

This book explores the aforementioned avenues and provides detailed information on how to initiate an export business through one of these approaches.

Government Support for Indian Exporters

India, with its vast population, diverse industries, and rich cultural heritage, has immense potential to be a global export powerhouse. To realize this potential, the Indian government has implemented various policies and initiatives to support exporters.

The Government of India plays a pivotal role in fostering India's export prowess and empowering Small and Medium Enterprises (SMEs) to venture into global markets. Through a multifaceted approach encompassing policy frameworks, financial incentives, and infrastructural development, the government strives to create a conducive environment for Indian exporters to thrive.

One of the cornerstones of government support is the formulation and implementation of sound export promotion policies. These policies aim to streamline export procedures, reduce bureaucratic hurdles, and provide a level playing field for Indian exporters. By simplifying customs clearances, reducing documentation requirements, and implementing efficient trade facilitation measures, the government ensures that exporters can focus on their core business activities without undue administrative burdens.

Financial incentives are another crucial component of government support for exporters. The government offers a range of schemes and subsidies to offset the costs associated with exporting, such as interest rate subsidies on export credit, duty drawback schemes, and export promotion capital goods schemes. These incentives provide much-needed financial support to exporters, especially SMEs, enabling them to compete effectively in global markets.

Recognizing the immense potential of SMEs in driving India's export growth, the government has undertaken several initiatives to encourage their participation in international trade. These initiatives include capacity-building programs, market intelligence services, and mentorship programs to equip SMEs with the necessary knowledge and skills to navigate the complexities of global trade. Additionally, the government has established specialized export promotion councils and export hubs to provide focused support and guidance to SMEs.

Infrastructure development is another key area where the government plays a crucial role in promoting exports. By investing in modern ports, airports, and logistics infrastructure, the government ensures efficient movement of goods and services, reducing logistics costs and improving India's overall export competitiveness. Furthermore, the government's emphasis on digital infrastructure and e-commerce platforms has facilitated seamless cross-border trade and enabled SMEs to reach global consumers directly.

Several government departments and agencies play a crucial role in promoting exports, including the Department of Commerce, the Directorate General of Foreign Trade (DGFT), the Federation of Indian Export Organisations (FIEO), and various Export Promotion Councils (EPCs). These entities work collaboratively to create a supportive environment for Indian exporters by formulating and implementing export promotion policies, simplifying customs procedures, providing financial incentives, and organizing trade fairs and exhibitions. Additionally, they offer market intelligence, capacity-building programs, and mentorship services to empower SMEs to compete effectively in global markets. Through these concerted efforts, the government aims to boost India's export potential and contribute to the nation's economic growth.

Here are some key Government organisations and agencies that play a crucial role in promoting exports:

- **Ministry of Commerce and Industry**—The Ministry of Commerce and Industry is the primary government department responsible for overseeing trade and commerce in India. It formulates and implements policies to promote exports and attract foreign investment.

- **Department of Commerce**—The Department of Commerce within the Ministry of Commerce and Industry is specifically tasked with promoting exports. It provides various services and support to exporters, including market intelligence, trade promotion, and policy advocacy.

- **Indian Trade Promotion Organization (ITPO)**—The ITPO is a statutory body under the Department of Commerce that organizes trade fairs, exhibitions, and buyer-seller meets to promote Indian exports. It also provides market information and assistance to exporters.

- **Export Credit Guarantee Corporation of India (ECGC)**—The ECGC is a government-backed financial institution that provides insurance cover against risks associated with exports, such as buyer insolvency and political risks.

- **Export-Import Bank of India (Exim Bank)**—The Exim Bank is a specialized financial institution that provides financial assistance to Indian exporters and importers. It offers a range of services, including export credit financing, project finance, and foreign investment promotion.

- **Directorate General of Foreign Trade (DGFT)**—The DGFT is the Indian government agency responsible for regulating foreign trade. It issues import and export licenses, notifies trade policies, and provides information to exporters and importers.

Government Initiatives and Schemes

The Indian government has made and is continuously making significant efforts to support exporters and promote Indian exports. By providing various incentives, services, and infrastructure, the government aims to create a conducive environment for Indian businesses to compete in the global market. While there are still challenges to be addressed, the government's commitment to supporting exports is evident. With continued efforts and a focused approach, India can become a major player in the global export market. Indian government has implemented numerous initiatives and schemes to support exporters:

- **Foreign Trade Policy (FTP)**—The FTP is the flagship policy document of the government that outlines the framework for promoting exports and attracting foreign investment. It provides various incentives and benefits to exporters, such as duty drawback, export promotion capital goods (EPCG) scheme, and Merchandise Exports from India Scheme (MEIS).

- **Export Promotion Capital Goods (EPCG) Scheme**—The EPCG scheme allows exporters to import capital goods at concessional customs duty rates if they are used for the export production of specified products.

- **Merchandise Exports from India Scheme (MEIS)**—The MEIS provides duty drawback benefits to exporters of specified products.

- **Export Promotion Council (EPCs)**—The government has established various Export Promotion Councils (EPCs) for specific product sectors, such as textiles, electronics, and chemicals. These EPCs provide sector-specific support and services to exporters.

- **Trade Fairs and Exhibitions**—The Indian government organizes and participates in numerous trade fairs and exhibitions both domestically and internationally to promote Indian exports and showcase the capabilities of Indian exporters.

- **Market Access Initiative (MAI)**—The MAI is a government initiative aimed at improving market access for Indian exporters by addressing trade barriers and negotiating favourable trade agreements.

- **Digital India Initiative**—The Digital India Initiative promotes the use of digital technologies in various sectors, including exports. It aims to improve efficiency, reduce costs, and enhance the competitiveness of Indian exporters.

- **Skill India Mission**—The Skill India Mission focuses on developing the skills of the Indian workforce, which is essential for producing high-quality products and services for export.

- **Make in India Initiative**—The Make in India Initiative aims to promote manufacturing and attract foreign investment in India. It can indirectly benefit exports by increasing the availability of domestically produced goods for export.

Export Promotion Councils (EPCs)

Export Promotion Councils (EPCs) are specialised organisations in India established to promote the export of specific products or sectors. Their primary role is to facilitate international trade by providing exporters with the necessary resources, guidance, and support to increase their competitiveness in global markets. EPCs work under the administrative control of the Ministry of Commerce and Industry, Government of India, and operate as non-profit entities.

Functions of EPCs

- **Market Intelligence and Research**: EPCs provide exporters with essential data and insights about global market trends, potential export destinations, and emerging opportunities. By offering periodic market reports and analysis, EPCs help exporters make informed business decisions.

- **Trade Shows and International Fairs**: EPCs organise or support participation in international trade shows, exhibitions, and buyer-seller meets. This provides exporters with opportunities to showcase their products, connect with potential buyers, and explore new markets.

- **Policy Advocacy**: EPCs represent exporters' interests and act as a bridge between the government and exporters. They advocate for policies that favour exports, provide feedback to the government on trade policies, and address exporters' issues through consultations and representations.

- **Export Incentive Guidance**: EPCs guide exporters on availing various government schemes and incentives, such as the Merchandise Exports from India Scheme (MEIS), Remission of Duties and Taxes on Exported Products (RoDTEP), and others. They help exporters understand eligibility criteria and assist with the application process.

- **Training and Skill Development**: EPCs organise training programmes, workshops, and seminars on topics such as international trade regulations, export documentation, product quality standards, and digital marketing. These initiatives help exporters build capacity and align with global best practices.

- **Product and Quality Certification Assistance**: EPCs help exporters meet international standards by providing guidance on quality certifications like ISO, BIS, and other industry-specific standards. Some councils also assist in obtaining certifications required for export to specific countries, such as the EU's CE mark for electronics or RoHS compliance.

- **Resolution of Trade Disputes**: EPCs offer support in resolving disputes that may arise in international trade. They mediate issues related to quality complaints, payment defaults, and logistical issues, helping exporters maintain business continuity.

- **Sector-Specific Support**: Each EPC focuses on a specific sector, such as textiles, gems and jewellery, engineering goods, or agricultural products. This specialisation enables them to address unique industry challenges, including regulatory requirements, product-specific standards, and target market preferences.

Presently, there are fourteen Export Promotion Councils under the administrative control of the Department of Commerce. These Councils are registered as non-profit organizations under the Companies Act/ Societies Registration Act. The Councils perform both advisory and executive functions. The role and functions of these Councils are guided by the Foreign Trade Policy, 2009-14. These Councils are also the registering authorities for exporters under the Foreign Trade Policy 2009-14.

- Basic Chemicals, Pharmaceuticals and Cosmetics Export Promotion Council (Chemexcil)
- Chemicals and Allied Products Export Promotion Council (CAPEXIL)
- Council for Leather Exports
- Sports Goods Export Promotion Council
- Gem and Jewellery Export Promotion Council

- Shellac Export Promotion Council
- Cashew Export Promotion Council of India
- The Plastics Export Promotion Council
- Export Promotion Council for EOUs & SEZ Units (EPCES)
- Pharmaceutical Export Promotion Council
- Indian Oil Seeds & Produce Export Promotion Council (IOPEPC)
- Services Export Promotion Council

In addition to the aforementioned fourteen Export Promotion Councils (EPCs), there are other EPCs operating in India. Please note that the specific number of EPCs may vary over time. For the most current list, it is recommended to consult the official website of the Department of Commerce, Ministry of Commerce and Industry, Government of India.

Subscription Charges for EPCs

The subscription fees and membership requirements for Export Promotion Councils vary depending on the council and the exporter's annual turnover or export volume. EPCs typically offer different membership categories such as "Associate Member" and "Ordinary Member," each with its fee structure. Here's an outline of the typical subscription charges and requirements. Please note that the charges indicated here are approximate and subject to change. For the most accurate and up-to-date information, kindly refer to the respective EPC websites.

- **One-Time Registration Fee:** Most EPCs charge a one-time registration or enrolment fee at the time of joining. This fee generally ranges from ₹2,000 to ₹10,000, depending on the council and the type of membership.

- **Annual Membership Fee:** Annual membership fees vary significantly by EPC and membership level.

- **Associate Member:** Usually applicable for smaller businesses or those with limited export turnover, with fees ranging from ₹5,000 to ₹10,000 per annum.

- **Ordinary Member:** Generally, for larger exporters with substantial export volume, with annual fees that may range from ₹10,000 to ₹25,000 or more.

- **Turnover-Based Membership Fee:** Some councils, such as the EEPC and FIEO, base membership fees on the export turnover of the company, meaning larger exporters may pay higher fees.

- **Special Fees for Additional Services:** Some EPCs charge additional fees for specific services, such as participation in trade fairs, product testing and certification, or personalised market reports.

- **Discounts and Concessions:** Many EPCs offer concessions on membership fees for startups, micro, small, and medium enterprises (MSMEs), or exporters from less-developed regions.

Benefits of Joining an EPCs

The membership fees and subscription charges for EPCs are considered investments by exporters because of the substantial benefits they provide, including:

- Access to international trade fairs and buyer-seller meets.
- Priority access to government export incentives.
- Sector-specific training and support for certification.
- Assistance in navigating complex international trade regulations.
- Market intelligence reports that aid in strategic decision-making.

Legal and Regulatory Requirements

Exporting products from India requires compliance with a broad framework of legal and regulatory requirements. These requirements encompass obtaining licenses, adhering to export policies, meeting product standards, fulfilling customs and documentation mandates, and ensuring adherence to international and domestic financial regulations.

It's important to understand that both manufacturers-turned-exporters who export their own products and traders who export products made by other manufacturers must comply with legal and regulatory requirements. However, if you're simply partnering with a manufacturer to help them export their products, you don't need to worry about these specific requirements.

Below is a structured list of the key legal and regulatory requirements that exporters must meet in India, each explained in detail.

- **Importer Exporter Code**: Issued by the Directorate General of Foreign Trade (DGFT), the IEC is a unique 10-digit code essential for engaging in international trade. Without it, an exporter cannot legally conduct export transactions. Apply online through the DGFT portal, submitting a PAN card, business address proof, and bank details. The IEC, once obtained, is valid for a lifetime.

- **Compliance with the Foreign Trade Policy (FTP)**: Managed by the DGFT, the FTP outlines rules, guidelines, and export incentives for various goods. The policy encourages exports in sectors like textiles, pharmaceuticals, and engineering.

- **Product Standards and Quality Control**: Applicable to goods in sensitive categories such as food, chemicals, and electronics.

- **Customs Documentation and Procedures**: Includes key documents such as Shipping Bill, Bill of Landing, Commercial Invoice, Packaging List, Certificate of Origin,

- **Adherence to Trade Agreements and Rules of Origin (ROO)**: India has trade agreements with ASEAN, SAARC, the EU, and other countries. The Rules of Origin establish criteria for national origin, allowing Indian products to benefit from reduced tariffs.

- **Goods and Services Tax (GST) Compliance**: Exports are zero-rated under GST, meaning exporters do not pay GST but must claim refunds for input taxes on raw materials.

- **Intellectual Property Rights (IPR) Protection**: Exporters must secure relevant patents, trademarks, or copyrights to protect products in international markets, especially for technology, pharmaceuticals, or branded goods.

- **Compliance with Environmental and Safety Standards**: Sensitive sectors, such as chemicals and electronics, have stringent safety standards under agreements like the Montreal Protocol and the Basel Convention.

- **Payment Compliance under the Foreign Exchange Management Act (FEMA)**: Regulated by the Reserve Bank of India (RBI), FEMA governs foreign exchange and cross-border payment protocols. Payment realisation within the prescribed period is essential.

- **Trade Finance and Insurance**: The Export Credit Guarantee Corporation of India (ECGC) offers trade insurance to mitigate risks associated with buyer non-payment and political instability. Pre-shipment and post-shipment finance are also essential to fund production and shipment.

- **Anti-Corruption and Anti-Money Laundering Compliance**: The Prevention of Money Laundering Act (PMLA) requires exporters to conduct due diligence, report suspicious transactions, and maintain accurate records.

- **Transport and Logistics Compliance**: Exporters select air, sea, or multimodal transport based on product requirements and costs, ensuring they meet international packaging, handling, and delivery standards.

- **Packaging and Labelling Requirements**: Goods require proper labelling and packaging to meet regulatory and consumer expectations in target markets. This is especially critical for products like food, pharmaceuticals, and cosmetics.

- **Export Promotion Council (EPC) Registration**: EPCs provide sector-specific support to Indian exporters. By registering, exporters can access market intelligence, participate in trade fairs, and gain export incentives.

- **Compliance with Indian Standards for Overseas Exporters**: Certain export products must align with standards overseen by the Bureau of Indian Standards (BIS). Exporters are required to ensure that goods meet both national and international standards for quality, safety, and performance.

- **Adherence to Product-Specific Regulations**: Compliance with regulations specific to certain export categories.

Navigating the Export Landscape

Exporting products can be a lucrative venture for businesses of all sizes. Whether you're a manufacturer looking to expand your market reach or a trader seeking to capitalize on international opportunities, understanding the necessary steps is crucial. Let's explore the various options available for exporting Indian products, focusing on the importance of certifications, licenses, and company setup.

Manufacturers can benefit greatly by exporting directly, gaining control over pricing, distribution, and brand recognition while accessing larger markets. Key advantages include increased revenue, market diversification, and enhanced brand visibility. Trading companies offer flexibility by sourcing products from various suppliers, mitigating risks, and adapting to trends. Partnering with manufacturers reduces costs, leverages production expertise, and ensures quicker market entry. Success relies on compliance, quality assurance, and strategic planning for logistics and risks.

Exporting as a Manufacturer

As a manufacturer-turned-exporter can significantly benefit from directly exporting your products to international markets. By bypassing intermediaries, you can enjoy greater control over pricing, distribution, and customer relationships. This autonomy allows you to optimize profit margins and build stronger brand recognition. Additionally, direct export can provide valuable insights into foreign markets, enabling you to tailor your products and services to meet specific consumer demands. Furthermore, direct exporting can foster long-term relationships with foreign buyers, leading to increased sales and market penetration.

As a manufacturer-turned-exporter you will have a direct advantage when it comes to exporting your products. By obtaining the requisite certifications and licenses, you can streamline the export process and ensure compliance with international standards. These certifications often validate product quality, safety, and sustainability, enhancing their appeal in foreign markets.

As a manufacturer-turned-exporter, the profits you generate are entirely yours. Additionally, you bear full responsibility for the investments made in producing high-quality products.

As a manufacturer-turned-exporter you will enjoy multiple benefits including:

- **Increased Revenue**—Exporting can significantly boost revenue by accessing larger markets and reaching new customer segments.

  For example, an Indian manufacturer of handmade carpets might struggle to sell their entire production domestically due to limited demand. By exporting their carpets to international markets, such as the United States or Europe, the manufacturer can access a much larger customer base and significantly increase their revenue. These markets often have a higher appreciation for handcrafted products and are willing to pay premium prices, allowing the manufacturer to generate substantial profits.

- **Market Diversification**—Reducing reliance on the domestic market can mitigate risks associated with economic fluctuations.

  For example, a company that primarily relies on the Indian domestic market for its sales might face challenges during economic downturns, such as decreased consumer spending and reduced demand for its products. However, by diversifying its revenue streams through exports, the company can mitigate these risks. If the domestic market experiences a slowdown, the company can still generate revenue from its international sales, helping to stabilize its overall financial performance.

- **Enhanced Brand Recognition**—Exporting can elevate brand visibility and reputation in international markets.

  For example, an Indian manufacturer of organic food products might struggle to establish brand recognition in the domestic market due to intense competition. However, by exporting their products to international markets, such as Europe or North America, where there is a growing demand for organic and sustainable food, the manufacturer can gain significant brand visibility and recognition. International certifications and awards can further enhance the brand's reputation and credibility, making it more attractive to foreign buyers.

- **Access to Advanced Technologies**—Exposure to global markets can drive innovation and facilitate the adoption of advanced technologies.

  For example, an Indian manufacturer of textiles might be exposed to new trends and technologies in international markets, such as sustainable fabric production or advanced weaving techniques. By adopting these innovations, the manufacturer can improve the quality and sustainability of their products, making them more competitive and appealing to global buyers. Additionally, exposure to international markets can encourage the manufacturer to invest in research and development, leading to the development of innovative textile products that cater to emerging consumer preferences.

- **Job Creation**—Increased exports often lead to higher demand for domestic production, creating jobs and contributing to economic growth.

  For example, an Indian manufacturer of leather goods might experience increased demand for their products due to growing exports to European markets. To meet this increased demand, the manufacturer may need to expand their production facilities, hire additional workers, and source more raw materials from domestic suppliers. This increased economic activity can contribute to job creation, stimulate local businesses, and overall boost the economy.

Since you are the manufacturer-turned-exporter, you may face some challenges in exporting from India

- **Bureaucratic Hurdles**—Navigating complex regulations, obtaining necessary permits, and dealing with administrative procedures can be time-consuming and challenging.

- **Infrastructure Constraints**—Inadequate infrastructure, such as transportation and logistics, can hinder the timely delivery of goods to foreign markets.

- **Quality Standards**—Adhering to international quality standards and certifications can be demanding, requiring significant investments in quality management systems.

- **Trade Barriers**—Tariffs, quotas, and non-tariff barriers imposed by importing countries can limit market access and increase costs.

- **Currency Fluctuations**—Fluctuations in the Indian rupee can impact the profitability of exports and make it difficult to plan pricing strategies.

As a manufacturer-turned-exporter, you must invest in the export-oriented aspects of your business, including:

- **Market Research**—Conduct thorough market research to identify potential export markets, understand consumer preferences, and assess competitive landscapes.

- **Product Development**—Ensure your products meet international quality standards and certifications. Consider customization to cater to specific market requirements.

- **Legal and Regulatory Compliance**—Obtain necessary licenses, permits, and registrations, such as the Import Export Code (IEC), Goods and Services Tax (GST) registrations and Registration-Cum-Membership Certificate (RCMC).

- **Export Documentation**—Prepare accurate and complete export documentation, including invoices, packing lists, bills of lading, and certificates of origin.

- **Packaging and labelling**—Ensure proper packaging and labelling to protect products during transit and comply with international regulations.

- **Transportation and Logistics**—Select reliable shipping partners and coordinate logistics arrangements for efficient transportation of goods.

- **Payment Terms and Risk Mitigation**—Negotiate favourable payment terms with foreign buyers and consider risk mitigation measures like export credit insurance.

- **After-Sales Service**—Provide excellent after-sales support to maintain customer satisfaction and build long-term relationships.

Exporting as a Trading Company

Even if you're not a manufacturer, you can still engage in the export business by setting up your own trading company. This involves a more administrative process, requiring you to obtain the necessary registrations and licenses. While it might be more time-consuming, establishing a trading company grants you greater flexibility and control over your export operations.

Exporting as a trading company can be a lucrative venture, offering opportunities to expand market reach, diversify revenue streams, and capitalize on international trade opportunities.

Establishing a trading company can be a strategic approach for businesses looking to engage in export activities. While manufacturing units offer direct control over production, trading companies provide distinct advantages in terms of flexibility, risk management, and market access.

- **Flexibility and Diversification**
  - <u>Product Range</u>—Trading companies can diversify their product offerings by sourcing from multiple manufacturers, catering to a wider range of customer preferences and market demands.

    For example, a trading company based in India could source textile products from various manufacturers across the country, including cotton, silk, and jute fabrics. This diversification allows the company to cater to a wider range of customer preferences, from budget-friendly cotton clothing to luxury silk garments. Additionally, by sourcing from multiple manufacturers, the trading company can ensure a continuous supply of products, even if one supplier faces disruptions.

- <u>Market Adaptation</u>—Trading companies have greater flexibility to adapt to market trends and changes in consumer preferences, allowing them to quickly introduce new products or adjust pricing strategies.

  For example, a trading company specializing in electronics could quickly adapt to the growing demand for smartphones by sourcing new models from different manufacturers and adjusting its product offerings. If the market for smartphones becomes saturated, the trading company can shift its focus to other electronic products, such as tablets or laptops, demonstrating its flexibility in responding to changing consumer preferences and market trends.

- <u>Risk Management</u>—By dealing with multiple suppliers, trading companies can mitigate risks associated with fluctuations in supply, quality, or pricing.

  For example, a trading company importing agricultural products from various regions in India can mitigate the risk of supply disruptions caused by factors such as adverse weather conditions or crop failures. By sourcing from multiple suppliers, the trading company can ensure a continuous supply of products, even if one supplier experiences difficulties. Additionally, dealing with multiple suppliers can provide greater flexibility in terms of pricing and quality, allowing the trading company to negotiate better terms and select the most suitable products for its customers.

- **Benefits of Exporting as a Trading Company**
  - <u>Market Diversification</u>—Trading companies can access a wider range of markets and products, reducing reliance on domestic demand.
  - <u>Profit Margins</u>—Trading can often yield higher profit margins compared to manufacturing due to reduced overhead costs.

- <u>Flexibility</u>—Trading companies have greater flexibility in terms of product selection, pricing, and market targeting.
- <u>Risk Management</u>—By dealing with multiple suppliers and buyers, trading companies can mitigate risks associated with fluctuations in demand or supply.
- <u>Knowledge Sharing</u>—Trading companies can leverage their expertise in international trade to assist manufacturers in expanding their export operations.

- **Challenges of Exporting as a Trading Company**
  - <u>Competition</u>—The global trading landscape is highly competitive, requiring trading companies to differentiate themselves based on product selection, pricing, and customer service.
  - <u>Market Research</u>—Identifying suitable export markets, understanding consumer preferences, and assessing competitive landscapes can be time-consuming and resource-intensive.
  - <u>Risk Management</u>—Managing risks such as currency fluctuations, political instability, and buyer insolvency is crucial for successful trading.
  - <u>Logistics and Supply Chain Management</u>—Ensuring efficient transportation, customs clearance, and supply chain management is essential for timely delivery of goods.
  - <u>Legal and Regulatory Compliance</u>—Adhering to complex export regulations, obtaining necessary licenses, and managing documentation can be challenging.

- **Essential Steps for Exporting as a Trading Company**
  - <u>Company Registration</u>—Register your trading company with the Registrar of Companies (RoC) and obtain an Import Export Code (IEC) from the Directorate General of Foreign Trade (DGFT).
  - <u>Market Research</u>—Conduct thorough market research to identify potential export markets, analyse consumer preferences, and assess competitive landscapes.

- <u>Product Sourcing</u>—Establish relationships with reliable manufacturers or suppliers who can provide quality products at competitive prices.

- <u>Export Documentation</u>—Prepare accurate and complete export documentation, including invoices, packing lists, bills of lading, and certificates of origin.

- <u>Negotiation and Contracting</u>—Negotiate favourable terms with suppliers and buyers, including pricing, payment terms, and delivery schedules.

- <u>Logistics and Shipping</u>—Arrange for efficient transportation and shipping of goods, ensuring compliance with customs regulations and international trade agreements.

- <u>Risk Management</u>—Implement risk mitigation strategies, such as export credit insurance and hedging against currency fluctuations.

- <u>After-Sales Service</u>—Provide excellent customer service and after-sales support to maintain relationships with buyers.

Partnering with Manufacturers

Partnering with manufacturers can be a strategic and efficient approach to entering the export market, particularly for those who do not have their own manufacturing capabilities or prefer to focus on sales and marketing. By collaborating with established manufacturers, you can leverage their production expertise, supply chain networks, and existing customer relationships to accelerate your export business.

Key Benefits of Partnering with Manufacturers

- **Reduced Initial Investment**—Partnering with manufacturers eliminates the need for significant upfront investments in manufacturing facilities, machinery, and labour. This can significantly reduce your capital outlay and operational costs.

- **Leveraging Manufacturing Expertise**—Manufacturers possess specialized knowledge and experience in production processes, quality control, and supply chain management. By partnering with them, you can benefit from their expertise and ensure the production of high-quality products.

- **Access to Established Supply Chains**—Manufacturers often have well-established supply chains, including reliable suppliers of raw materials and components. This can streamline your procurement process and reduce lead times.

- **Market Access**—Many manufacturers have existing distribution networks and customer relationships in international markets. By partnering with them, you can gain access to these markets more quickly and efficiently.

- **Focus on Core Competencies**—Partnering allows you to focus on your core competencies, such as sales, marketing, and customer relationship management. This can enhance your ability to identify and capitalize on new market opportunities.

Key Considerations for Successful Partnerships

- **Clear Partnership Agreement**—A well-defined partnership agreement is crucial to outline the roles, responsibilities, and expectations of both parties. It should cover aspects such as product specifications, pricing, payment terms, quality control, intellectual property rights, and dispute resolution mechanisms.

- **Effective Communication**—Open and transparent communication is essential for a successful partnership. Regular communication can help to resolve issues promptly, build trust, and ensure that both parties are aligned on their goals.

- **Quality Assurance**—Implementing robust quality control measures is vital to maintain product quality and customer satisfaction. Collaborate with the manufacturer to establish quality standards and inspection procedures.

- **Risk Management**—Identify potential risks, such as supply chain disruptions, currency fluctuations, and political instability, and develop strategies to mitigate them.

- **Legal and Regulatory Compliance**—Ensure compliance with export regulations, customs procedures, and international trade agreements. This includes obtaining necessary licenses, permits, and certifications.

- **Financial Considerations**—Establish clear financial terms, including pricing, payment terms, and profit-sharing arrangements. Consider factors such as currency exchange rates and potential fluctuations.

By carefully selecting partners, establishing clear communication channels, and implementing effective risk management strategies, you can build strong and mutually beneficial partnerships that drive export success.

Comparison of Exporting Strategies: Manufacturer, Trading Company, and Partnering with Manufacturers

This table highlights the key differences between each export strategy, emphasizing the benefits and challenges associated with each.

Aspect	Exporting as a Manufacturer	Exporting as a Trading Company	Partnering with Manufacturers
Control	High control over production, pricing, and distribution.	Less control over production, more control over product sourcing and pricing.	Limited control over production, focus on sales and marketing.
Investment	Requires significant investment in production	Requires investment in administrative processes,	Reduced initial investment by leveraging the manufacturer's resources.

Aspect	Exporting as a Manufacturer	Exporting as a Trading Company	Partnering with Manufacturers
	facilities and processes.	licensing, and registration.	
Revenue	Full profits from sales.	Profits based on sourcing and trading margin, often higher due to reduced overhead.	Profit sharing depending on agreement with the manufacturer.
Risk	Bear full responsibility for production and quality.	Risks related to supply disruptions, market fluctuations, and logistics.	Risks shared with the manufacturer, though some market risks remain.
Market Reach	Limited to product-specific markets unless diversified.	Can diversify product range and market reach more flexibly.	Quick market access using the manufacturer's established networks.
Certifications and Compliance	Requires meeting international standards and certifications for products.	Must adhere to trade regulations and certifications, but no production-related certifications needed.	Rely on the manufacturer for compliance but must ensure trade documentation is correct.
Innovation and Technology	Direct exposure to global trends and innovations in the manufacturing sector.	Flexibility to switch between products based on trends and market needs.	Rely on the manufacturer's technology and innovation but can benefit from their expertise.

Aspect	Exporting as a Manufacturer	Exporting as a Trading Company	Partnering with Manufacturers
Job Creation	Leads to job creation by expanding production facilities.	May not directly impact job creation, as it focuses more on trade than production.	Potential job creation within the trading company, but less than manufacturing.
Bureaucratic Challenges	Must navigate complex export regulations and certifications.	Must manage complex trade regulations, permits, and licenses.	Focus on compliance with international trade regulations, leveraging the manufacturer's knowledge.
Flexibility in Product Offering	Less flexibility as tied to own manufacturing capabilities.	High flexibility in product sourcing and adapting to market demands.	Moderate flexibility, depending on the manufacturer's offerings.
After-Sales Service	Direct responsibility for after-sales support and customer relations.	Responsible for after-sales service, relying on manufacturers for product issues.	Limited responsibility for after-sales, as the manufacturer handles product issues.
Market Diversification	Dependent on the manufacturer's ability to diversify products and markets.	Easier diversification through sourcing from various suppliers.	Dependent on the manufacturer's existing market networks and product range.

Aspect	Exporting as a Manufacturer	Exporting as a Trading Company	Partnering with Manufacturers
Infrastructure and Logistics	Full responsibility for logistics, packaging, and shipping.	Must ensure efficient logistics and customs management but has flexibility in shipping partners.	Relies on the manufacturer for supply chain and logistics expertise.

Roles of Freight Forwarders and CHAs

When exporting goods internationally, two key players often come into the picture: freight forwarders and customs house agents. These professionals play crucial roles in ensuring smooth and efficient transportation and clearance of goods across borders.

Freight Forwarders

A freight forwarder is essentially a logistics expert who organizes the transportation of goods from the point of origin to the final destination. They act as intermediaries between the exporter and various carriers, such as shipping lines, airlines, and trucking companies.

Key Roles of a Freight Forwarder

- **Booking Cargo Space**: They negotiate with carriers to secure the best rates and shipping schedules for the exporter's goods.

- **Documentation**: They handle the preparation of necessary shipping documents, including bills of lading, packing lists, and commercial invoices.

- **Customs Clearance (Export)**: While they may not handle the specific customs clearance process themselves, they can assist in preparing the required documentation and coordinating with customs brokers.

- **Tracking Shipments**: They monitor the progress of shipments and provide updates to the exporter.

- **Insurance**: They can arrange for insurance coverage to protect the goods during transit.

Example: If an Indian exporter wants to ship a container of textiles to the United States, a freight forwarder would:

- **Book Shipping Space**: Negotiate with a shipping line to secure space on a container ship sailing from an Indian port to a US port.

- **Coordinate Pickup**: Arrange for the pickup of the goods from the exporter's warehouse and transport them to the port.

- **Prepare Documentation**: Create necessary shipping documents, such as the bill of lading and packing list.

- **Handle Customs Clearance (Export)**: Assist the exporter in preparing the required customs documentation and ensuring compliance with export regulations.

- **Track Shipment**: Monitor the shipment's progress and provide updates to the exporter.

Custom House Agents

A customs house agent, also known as a customs broker, specializes in handling customs procedures. They are licensed professionals who are well-versed in customs laws, regulations, and procedures.

Key Roles of a Custom House Agent

- **Customs Clearance (Import and Export)**: They prepare and submit the necessary customs declarations, pay duties and taxes, and handle any customs inspections.

- **Documentation**: They ensure that all required documents are accurate and complete.

- **Compliance**: They help exporters and importers comply with customs regulations and avoid penalties.

Example: For the same textile shipment to the US, a customs house agent in the US would:

- **Prepare Customs Declarations**: Create the necessary customs declaration forms, including the Customs Importer Security Filing (ISF) and Entry Summary.

- **Clear Customs**: Submit the customs declaration to US Customs and Border Protection (CBP) and handle any inspections or inquiries.

- **Pay Duties and Taxes**: Calculate and pay any applicable duties and taxes on the imported goods.

- **Release the Shipment**: Once the customs clearance process is complete, the agent arranges for the release of the goods from customs custody.

By utilizing the services of freight forwarders and customs house agents, exporters can streamline the complex process of international shipping and ensure that their goods reach their destination efficiently and compliantly.

Selecting & Procuring Products to Export

As a trading company or partner of a manufacturing firm, you have the flexibility to curate a diverse product portfolio for export, selecting items that align with market demand and profitability. Conversely, as a manufacturer transitioning into exporting, your initial focus should be on leveraging your existing production capabilities. Prioritize exporting products that align with your core competencies and manufacturing strengths. This strategic approach ensures a seamless transition into international markets while optimizing resource utilization.

You are an Indian exporter and you should know what India exports. While deciding on which products to export find out the product trends over the recent years, the export growth in past few years and the respective values in USD. If the product was in demand in the previous years, they may be in demand in future too. Its however an estimation. As a partner of manufacturing company or a trader you can quicky shift your export focus on in-demand products.

You will be able to get information on in-demand products from a variety of sources including DGFT, Trademap, Volza among others. DGFT is an Indian government site and provides information on how much export is done from India in a particular year for a particular HSN code.

Selecting the right products for export from India is a crucial step in building a successful international business. By carefully considering various factors, you can identify products that have high demand in global markets and align with your business goals. Here's a detailed guide to help you make informed decisions:

* **Identify Your Niche**
    - <u>Leverage India's Strengths</u>: India is renowned for its diverse industries, including textiles, handicrafts, pharmaceuticals, IT services, and agricultural products. Consider focusing on sectors where India has a competitive advantage.

- Market Research: Conduct thorough market research to identify specific product categories with high demand in your target markets.
- Competitive Analysis: Analyse your competitors' product offerings to identify gaps and opportunities.

- **Product Selection Criteria**
  - High Demand: Choose products with consistent global demand.
  - Profit Margin: Ensure that the product offers a reasonable profit margin after considering production costs, shipping, and import duties.
  - Shelf Life: Opt for products with a long shelf life to minimize losses during transportation and storage.
  - Easy to Ship: Prioritize products that are easy to package and ship, especially if you're dealing with international logistics.
  - Compliance with Regulations: Ensure that your products comply with international quality and safety standards, as well as import and export regulations.

- **Consider Your Target Market**
  - Cultural Sensitivity: Understand the cultural preferences and sensitivities of your target market.
  - Consumer Preferences: Research the specific needs and preferences of your target consumers.
  - Local Regulations: Familiarize yourself with the import regulations and customs procedures of your target market.

- **Evaluate Your Manufacturing Capabilities**
  - Production Capacity: Assess your production capacity to meet potential export orders.
  - Quality Control: Implement strict quality control measures to ensure consistent product quality.

- **Leverage Government Support**
  - <u>Export Promotion Councils (EPCs)</u>: These councils provide valuable assistance, including market information, export financing, and guidance on export procedures.
  - <u>Export Credit Guarantee Corporation (ECGC)</u>: ECGC offers insurance coverage to mitigate risks associated with export transactions.
  - <u>State-Level Export Promotion Agencies</u>: Many states in India have dedicated export promotion agencies that can offer support and incentives.

- **Build Strong Relationships**
  - <u>Network with Importers and Distributors</u>: Develop strong relationships with importers and distributors in your target markets.
  - <u>Attend Trade Fairs and Exhibitions</u>: Participate in international trade events to connect with potential buyers and partners.
  - <u>Utilize Online Marketplaces</u>: Leverage online platforms like Alibaba, Amazon, and eBay to reach a global audience.

By carefully considering these factors and following a systematic approach, you can identify and export products that are in high demand, profitable, and align with your business goals.

Setting Up a Company to Export Products

The information provided regarding company formation is based on current government policies and regulations. For accurate and up-to-date guidance, it is advisable to consult with a Chartered Accountant.

Here we will discuss what are the different types of companies that you can set up for your export business and their advantages and disadvantages.

Proprietorship Company

A sole proprietorship is a business owned and managed by a single individual. It is suitable for small-scale businesses with minimal investment. The sole proprietor has complete control over the business and enjoys all the profits. However, they also bear full responsibility for all business losses and liabilities.

While a proprietorship is a simple and easy-to-establish business structure, it presents certain limitations, particularly in the context of export business:

- **Unlimited Liability**—One of the major drawbacks of a proprietorship is the unlimited liability of the owner. This means that the owner's personal assets are at risk in case of business debts or legal liabilities. This can be particularly risky in international trade, where unforeseen circumstances and legal complexities can arise.

- **Limited Capital**—Proprietorships often have limited access to capital, which can hinder their ability to invest in growth, expand operations, or manage unforeseen challenges. This can be a significant limitation in the export business, where substantial investments may be required for logistics, marketing, and compliance.

- **Lack of Continuity**—A proprietorship's existence is tied to the life of the owner. If the owner dies or becomes incapacitated, the business may face disruption or even dissolution. This can negatively impact long-term export strategies and customer relationships.

- **Limited Credibility**—In international trade, credibility and trust are crucial. A proprietorship, as a single-person business, may not have the same level of credibility as a larger, established company. This can make it difficult to secure deals with foreign buyers and suppliers.

- **Regulatory Challenges**—While the regulatory requirements for setting up a proprietorship are relatively simple, compliance with export regulations, customs procedures, and international trade laws can be complex. Navigating these regulations can be more challenging for a sole proprietor without dedicated legal and compliance teams.

To mitigate these disadvantages, it is recommended to opt for more structured business structures like a Private Limited Company or a Limited Liability Partnership (LLP), which offer limited liability protection and greater credibility in the international market.

The proprietorship is the simplest form of business structure in India. It doesn't require any legal formalities or registrations beyond a few essential steps.

One Person Company (OPC)

One Person Company (OPC) was introduced in the Companies Act, 2013. As the name suggests, an OPC is incorporated by a single individual who both establishes and manages it. Possessing the characteristics of a company, including perpetual succession, limited liability, and a distinct legal entity status, OPCs offer several advantages. These include legal recognition, the ability to raise funds, reduced compliance burdens, ease of setup and management, and the option to appoint a nominee as a successor in case of the owner's demise.

However, OPCs are primarily suited for small businesses and may have limitations in terms of expansion and growth. Due to the single-person structure, clients may prefer to work with companies that offer greater assurance of continuity and stability. Therefore, OPCs may not be the ideal choice for serious export businesses.

While One Person Companies (OPCs) offer several advantages, they also have certain limitations, particularly for export businesses:

- **Limited Capital Raising**—While OPCs can raise funds by issuing shares, the scope for raising significant capital is limited compared to larger company structures like public limited companies. This can hinder large-scale export operations that require substantial investments.

- **Regulatory Compliance**—While OPCs have simplified compliance procedures compared to larger companies, they still require adherence to various regulatory requirements, including filing annual returns, conducting board meetings, and maintaining statutory records. Non-compliance with these regulations can lead to penalties and legal consequences.

- **Limited Managerial Capacity**—For large-scale export operations, a single person may find it challenging to manage all aspects of the business, including sourcing, production, marketing, finance, and logistics. This can lead to operational inefficiencies and hinder growth.

- **Perception of Limited Scale**—Some international partners may perceive OPCs as smaller, less established businesses, which could impact their willingness to engage in large-scale transactions or long-term partnerships.

- **Succession Planning**—While OPCs allow for the appointment of a nominee shareholder, succession planning can still be complex, especially if the nominee lacks the necessary expertise or experience to manage the business.

To address these limitations, it is recommended to consider transitioning to a private limited company or a limited liability partnership as their business grows and expands. These structures offer greater flexibility, scalability, and credibility in the international market.

Limited Liability Partnership (LLP) Company

A Limited Liability Partnership (LLP) is a hybrid form of business organization that combines the features of a partnership and a company. It provides the flexibility of a partnership with the limited liability protection of a company. This structure has gained popularity among exporters in India due to its numerous advantages.

- **Key Features of an LLP**
  - <u>Separate Legal Entity</u>—An LLP is a distinct legal entity, separate from its partners.
  - <u>Limited Liability</u>—The liability of partners is limited to their capital contribution.
  - <u>Flexible Structure</u>—LLPs offer flexibility in terms of profit sharing, management, and decision-making.
  - <u>Ease of Formation and Management</u>—The process of setting up and managing an LLP is relatively simple compared to other corporate structures.
  - <u>Tax Benefits</u>—LLPs enjoy certain tax benefits, such as lower tax rates and easier tax compliance.

- **Advantages of LLP Over OPC for Exporters**

  While OPCs offer several benefits, LLPs have certain advantages that make them a more suitable choice for exporters:

  - <u>Enhanced Credibility and Trust</u>
    - Multiple Partners—An LLP typically involves multiple partners, which can enhance credibility and trust among international clients and partners.
    - Professional Image—The formal structure of an LLP can project a more professional image, especially when dealing with foreign businesses.
  - <u>Greater Flexibility and Scalability</u>
    - Multiple Partners—LLPs can accommodate multiple partners, enabling them to pool resources, expertise, and networks.

- o Scalability—As the business grows, LLPs can easily adapt and scale their operations, making them suitable for expanding export businesses.

- <u>Effective Risk Management</u>
  - o Shared Liability—The liability of each partner is limited to their capital contribution, reducing individual risk exposure.
  - o Diversified Expertise—Multiple partners can bring diverse skills and expertise to the business, enhancing decision-making and risk management.

- <u>Tax Benefits</u>
  - o Lower Tax Rates—LLPs may enjoy lower tax rates compared to other corporate structures.
  - o Tax Planning Opportunities—The flexible structure of LLPs allows for effective tax planning and optimization.

- <u>Ease of Administration</u>
  - o Simplified Compliance—LLPs have relatively simpler compliance requirements compared to traditional companies, reducing administrative burdens.
  - o Flexible Management—LLPs offer flexibility in management, allowing partners to share responsibilities and make decisions collectively.

To set up an LLP for export business, follow these steps:

1. **Choose Partners**—Identify individuals or entities who will be partners in the LLP.

2. **Draft the Partnership Deed**—Prepare a partnership deed outlining the rights, duties, and responsibilities of each partner.

3. **Obtain Digital Signature Certificates (DSC)**—All designated partners must obtain DSCs.

   A Digital Signature Certificate (DSC) is the electronic equivalent of a handwritten signature. It's a secure digital file issued by a trusted Certifying Authority (CA) that verifies the identity of an individual or organization.

4. **File Incorporation Documents**—File the incorporation documents, including the partnership deed, with the Registrar of Companies (RoC).

5. **Obtain DIN**—Obtain a Director Identification Number (DIN) for each designated partner.

6. **Obtain PAN**—Obtain a Permanent Account Number (PAN) for the LLP.

7. **Open a Bank Account**—Open a bank account in the name of the LLP.

8. **Obtain Necessary Licenses and Permits**—Obtain licenses and permits required for export activities, such as an Import Export Code (IEC).

9. **Comply with Regulatory Requirements**—Adhere to regulatory requirements, including filing annual returns, conducting board meetings, and maintaining statutory records.

By carefully following these steps and considering the unique advantages of LLPs, exporters can establish a strong foundation for their business and achieve sustainable growth.

Private Limited Company

A Private Limited Company (PLC) is a popular corporate structure in India, offering a balance of flexibility and liability protection. For exporters, a PLC provides a strong foundation to build and scale their businesses.

- **Key Features of a Private Limited Company**
  - Separate Legal Entity—A PLC is a separate legal entity, distinct from its shareholders.
  - Limited Liability—The liability of shareholders is limited to the amount of capital they have invested in the company.
  - Perpetual Succession—A PLC can continue to exist even if shareholders change.

- <u>Flexible Capital Structure</u>—PLCs can raise capital through issuing shares to shareholders.

- **Advantages of a Private Limited Company Over LLP for Exporters**

While LLPs offer certain benefits, a Private Limited Company provides several advantages that make it a more suitable choice for many exporters:

- <u>Enhanced Credibility and Trust</u>
  - o Professional Image—A PLC is perceived as a more formal and established business entity, which can enhance credibility and trust among international partners.
  - o Investor Confidence—PLCs can attract investment from a wider range of investors, including venture capitalists and private equity firms.

- <u>Greater Flexibility and Scalability</u>
  - o Complex Corporate Structures—PLCs can adopt complex corporate structures, including subsidiaries and holding companies, to facilitate expansion and diversification.
  - o Access to Capital Markets—PLCs can raise capital through issuing shares to the public, providing a significant advantage for large-scale export operations.

- <u>Strong Legal Protection</u>
  - o Limited Liability—The limited liability feature of PLCs protects shareholders from personal liability for business debts.
  - o Perpetual Succession—PLCs can continue to exist indefinitely, ensuring business continuity and stability.

- <u>Clear Governance Structure</u>
  - o Board of Directors—PLCs have a board of directors responsible for strategic decision-making, providing a formal governance structure.

- o Professional Management—PLCs can hire professional managers to oversee day-to-day operations, allowing the owners to focus on strategic initiatives.

- Tax Benefits and Incentives
  - o Tax Advantages—PLCs may be eligible for various tax benefits and incentives, depending on specific government policies and industry regulations.

To set up a Private Limited Company in India, follow these steps:

1. **Digital Signature Certificates (DSC)**—Obtain DSCs for the proposed directors.
2. **Director Identification Number (DIN)** —Apply for DINs for the proposed directors.
3. **Name Approval**—File a name application with the Registrar of Companies (RoC) for the company name.
4. **Memorandum of Association (MoA)** —Draft the MoA, outlining the company's objectives and capital structure.
5. **Articles of Association (AoA)** —Draft the AoA, detailing the company's internal rules and regulations.
6. **Stamp Duty Payment**—Pay the required stamp duty.
7. **File Incorporation Documents**—File the incorporation documents, including the MoA, AoA, and other necessary forms, with the RoC.
8. **Certificate of Incorporation**—Upon approval, the RoC will issue a Certificate of Incorporation, signifying the company's legal existence.

A Private Limited Company offers a robust and flexible structure for export businesses. By understanding the advantages and following the necessary steps, exporters can establish a strong foundation for their ventures and achieve sustainable growth.

However, it's important to note that setting up and managing a PLC involves more complexities and compliance requirements compared to a proprietorship or LLP. Consulting with legal and tax professionals can help navigate the process effectively.

Comparison of Business Structures for Export Businesses in A Nutshell

This table captures the main aspects of each business structure in terms of suitability for export businesses, scalability, regulatory requirements, and other key factors.

Aspect	Proprietor-ship	One Person Company (OPC)	Limited Liability Partnership (LLP)	Private Limited Company (PLC)
Ownership	Sole proprietor, individual ownership	Owned and managed by a single person	Multiple partners, shared ownership	Owned by shareholders
Legal Entity	Not a separate legal entity	Separate legal entity	Separate legal entity	Separate legal entity
Liability	Unlimited liability, personal assets at risk	Limited liability, personal assets protected	Limited liability, partners only liable for capital invested	Limited liability, personal assets protected
Continuity	Dependent on the life of the owner	Perpetual succession , can appoint nominee	Perpetual succession	Perpetual succession
Capital Raising	Limited access to capital	Limited ability to raise capital	Can raise capital through additional partners	Can raise capital through issuing shares, access to capital markets
Growth & Scalability	Limited ability to scale	Limited capacity for growth	Flexible and scalable, can accommodate	Highly scalable, can raise large

Aspect	Proprietor-ship	One Person Company (OPC)	Limited Liability Partnership (LLP)	Private Limited Company (PLC)
		due to single-person structure	multiple partners	amounts of capital
Regulatory Compliance	Simple, minimal regulatory requirements	Simplified compliance but still requires filings	Moderate compliance, annual returns, and statutory records	High compliance, regular filings, board meetings, audits
Management & Operations	Managed by the owner	Managed by the owner with some flexibility for nominees	Flexible management structure, shared responsibilities	Board of Directors, professional management team
Credibility & Trust	Limited, may struggle with international partners	Perceived as smaller, may lack credibility in export business	Higher credibility due to multiple partners	High credibility, perceived as formal and established
Taxation	Simple, but higher tax burden due to lack of benefits	Simplified taxation, may still face certain limitations	Tax benefits, flexible structure for tax planning	Tax incentives and benefits available depending on policies
Succession Planning	Difficult, business ceases on owner's death	Allows for a nominee, but may be complex	Succession planning possible with multiple partners	Clear succession planning with shareholders and directors
Perceived Business Size	Small, may be perceived as less credible	Small, single-person structure	Seen as more professional	Perceived as established and large-scale, suitable

Aspect	Proprietorship	One Person Company (OPC)	Limited Liability Partnership (LLP)	Private Limited Company (PLC)
		may not appeal for large-scale export	with multiple partners	for bigger export businesses
Suitability for Export Business	Not recommended due to limited resources and liability risks	Limited scalability and capital raising, may struggle with large-scale exports	Suitable for exporters seeking flexibility and scalability	Best suited for large-scale export operations, strong international presence
Ease of Setup	Very easy, minimal formalities	Simple setup, but requires adherence to legal formalities	Moderate complexity, requires drafting partnership deed and legal documents	More complex setup, requires legal documentation and registration

Tips for Selecting a Bank for Your Export Business

Irrespective of whatever type of company you set up for your export business, you must have a bank account especially if you are setting up your export business as a manufacturer or a trading company. If you decide to partner with a manufacturer, you will be able to use your existing saving account to get your dues from the manufacturer. However, if you are setting up your export business as a manufacturer or a trading company you must have a current account in a bank. Here are some tips on how to choose a bank for your export business:

Selecting the right bank for your export business is a crucial decision that can significantly impact your operations and financial success. Here are key factors to consider when making this choice:

- **Authorised Dealer (AD) Category**

    - <u>Essential for Export-Import</u>: Ensure the bank holds an Authorised Dealer (AD) category license from the Reserve Bank of India (RBI). This license authorizes them to deal in foreign exchange and handle international trade transactions.

        RBI grants AD Category-I licenses to select banks to carry out all permissible current and capital account transactions.

        Here are some of the major banks in India that hold AD Category-I licenses. Note that the following banks are listed for illustrative purposes only and do not represent in any particular order.

Public Sector Banks	Private Sector Banks
State Bank of India (SBI)	HDFC Bank
Bank of Baroda	ICICI Bank
Punjab National Bank (PNB)	Axis Bank
Canara Bank	Kotak Mahindra Bank
Bank of India	IndusInd Bank

Public Sector Banks	Private Sector Banks
Bank of India	Yes Bank
Union Bank of India	Federal Bank
Indian Bank	IDFC First Bank
Bank of Maharashtra	
Central Bank of India	
UCO Bank	
Indian Overseas Bank	

To get the most accurate and up-to-date information, you can:

– Check the RBI's official website: The RBI's website provides detailed information on authorized dealers and their functions.

– Consult with your bank: Your bank can provide specific information about its AD category license and the services it offers.

– Seek advice from a financial advisor: A financial advisor can help you choose the best bank for your specific needs.

By choosing a bank with an AD Category-I license, you can ensure that your export-transactions are handled efficiently and in compliance with all relevant regulations.

♦ **Global Reach and Network**

– International Presence: Opt for a bank with a strong global network and correspondent banking relationships. This facilitates smooth cross-border transactions, especially for letters of credit (LCs) and remittances.

Foreign Exchange Services: A wide range of foreign exchange services, including currency exchange, remittances, and hedging instruments, can be beneficial for managing currency risks.

- **Trade Finance Expertise**

  - <u>Letter of Credit (LC) Facilitation</u>: Choose a bank with expertise in LCs can streamline the process, ensuring timely payments and mitigating risks.

    A Letter of Credit (LC) is a payment guarantee from the buyer's bank to the seller, ensuring payment upon the shipment of goods and submission of required documents. It is used in international trade to mitigate credit risks, particularly with new or high-risk buyers. LCs can be costly and require meticulous documentation. The process involves the buyer applying through their bank, document verification, and payment release upon compliance. They provide security for both parties but necessitate careful handling due to potential errors and fees.

  - <u>Export Credit Financing</u>: Choose a bank that offers export financial support.

    Several Indian banks offer export credit financing to support exporters. Note that the following banks are listed for illustrative purposes only and do not represent in any particular order. Here are some of the major ones:

Bank	Description
State Bank of India (SBI)	Offers a range of export finance products, including pre-shipment and post-shipment credit, export bills discounting, and export credit guarantees.
Bank of Baroda	Provides export credit facilities in both Indian Rupees and foreign currencies.
Punjab National Bank (PNB)	Offers pre-shipment and post-shipment credit, export bill discounting, and export credit guarantees.
Bank of India	Provides export finance solutions, including pre-shipment credit, post-shipment credit, and export bill discounting.
Canara Bank	Offers export credit facilities to support exporters, including pre-shipment and post-shipment credit.

Bank	Description
HDFC Bank	Provides a range of export finance solutions, including pre-shipment and post-shipment credit, export bill discounting, and export credit guarantees.
ICICI Bank	Offers export finance solutions, including pre-shipment and post-shipment credit, export bill discounting, and export credit guarantees.
Axis Bank	Provides export finance solutions, including pre-shipment and post-shipment credit, export bill discounting, and export credit guarantees.

Additionally, Exim Bank is a specialized financial institution that provides a wide range of financial products and services to promote India's foreign trade. They offer various export credit financing schemes to support exporters.

- **Digital Banking Capabilities**
  - <u>Online Banking</u>: A robust online banking platform with features like international fund transfers, real-time tracking, and secure document uploads can streamline your operations.
  - <u>Mobile Banking</u>: Mobile banking apps can provide convenient access to your accounts and enable you to conduct transactions on the go.

- **Customer Support and Service**
  - <u>Dedicated Trade Finance Team</u>: A dedicated team can provide expert guidance and support for your export-import needs.
  - <u>Prompt Response Time</u>: Efficient customer service is crucial for timely resolution of queries and issues.

- **Fees and Charges**
  - <u>Transparent Fee Structure</u>: Understand the bank's fee structure, including charges for foreign exchange transactions, LCs, and other services.

- — **Competitive Pricing:** Compare fees with other banks to ensure you're getting the best deal.

- ◆ **Security and Compliance**

  - • <u>Robust Security Measures</u>: The bank should have strong security measures in place to protect your financial information.

  - • <u>Compliance with Regulations</u>: Ensure the bank is compliant with all relevant regulations, including Know Your Customer (KYC) and Anti-Money Laundering (AML) norms.

How to Choose the Right Bank

- ◆ **Research:** Identify banks with a strong track record in international trade.

- ◆ **Compare Services:** Evaluate the range of services offered, including trade finance, foreign exchange, and digital banking.

- ◆ **Visit Branches:** Visit branches to assess the infrastructure, staff expertise, and overall customer experience.

- ◆ **Seek Recommendations:** Consult with other exporters or industry experts for recommendations.

- ◆ **Negotiate Fees:** Don't hesitate to negotiate fees and charges based on your transaction volume and relationship with the bank.

By carefully considering these factors, you can select a bank that will be a valuable partner in your export business, helping you navigate the complexities of international trade and achieve your growth objectives.

Preparing Yourself for Export Success

Before diving into the world of exporting, take the time to prepare yourself by reading books, attending workshops, and taking online courses to enhance your understanding of international trade and export procedures.

Make sure that you network with industry professionals, experienced exporters, industry experts, and government officials to gain valuable insights and advice. Some of the best online platforms to expand your network and connect with industry leaders.

Networking, a cornerstone of professional success, has evolved significantly in the digital age. While traditional methods still hold value, online platforms have revolutionized the way we connect with like-minded individuals. By leveraging these tools and adopting effective strategies, one can build a robust network that opens doors to new opportunities.

A crucial first step is to optimize your online profile. Ensure that your profile on platforms like LinkedIn and Twitter is accurate, up-to-date, and showcases your skills and experience. A well-crafted profile serves as a digital resume, attracting potential connections. To foster meaningful relationships, active engagement is paramount. Regularly participate in discussions, share insightful content, and respond promptly to messages. This demonstrates your interest and commitment to the community.

Joining relevant industry groups and communities is another effective way to connect with professionals in your field. These groups provide a platform for knowledge sharing, collaboration, and networking. Attending virtual or in-person events, such as conferences, webinars, and industry gatherings, offers opportunities to meet people face-to-face, exchange ideas, and build rapport.

After connecting with someone, it's essential to follow up with a personalized message. This reinforces your connection, expresses genuine interest, and sets the stage for future interactions. By utilizing these online platforms and following these tips, you can effectively network with industry professionals, expand your knowledge, and advance your career.

In the realm of international trade, networking plays a pivotal role in building strong relationships with potential buyers, suppliers, and logistics providers. These relationships are crucial for smooth operations, efficient supply chains, and successful exports. A well-crafted business plan is essential to guide your export endeavours. It should outline your specific goals, target markets, marketing strategies, financial projections, and risk mitigation plans.

By combining effective networking strategies with a solid business plan, you can navigate the complexities of international trade and achieve sustainable growth. Remember, networking is an ongoing process that requires consistent effort and genuine engagement. By investing time and energy in building strong relationships, you can unlock countless opportunities and propel your business to new heights.

Professional Networking

Professional networking platforms have revolutionized the way individuals connect and collaborate in the professional world. LinkedIn, the most prominent platform, empowers users to create comprehensive profiles, establish connections with colleagues, engage in industry-specific groups, and participate in insightful discussions. This platform fosters professional growth by facilitating knowledge sharing and career advancement opportunities.

LinkedIn is the world's largest professional networking platform, connecting individuals and businesses across diverse industries globally. For exporters, LinkedIn serves as a powerful tool to identify and engage with potential international buyers. By leveraging its advanced search filters, exporters can target specific industries, companies, and key decision-makers in desired markets. Additionally, LinkedIn enables professionals to showcase their products, services, and expertise through a well-crafted profile, posts, and articles, enhancing brand visibility and credibility.

Exporters can join relevant groups, participate in discussions, and connect with global trade professionals to stay informed about market trends and opportunities. The platform also offers features like InMail, which allows direct communication with prospects, and LinkedIn Sales Navigator, designed for lead generation and relationship building. By utilising LinkedIn effectively, exporters can expand their network, establish trust with potential buyers, and access a broader marketplace, ultimately driving business growth and international expansion.

For those interested in exporting to Europe, Xing offers a similar experience to LinkedIn, providing company profiles, job postings, and event listings. This platform caters to the specific needs of European professionals, making it a valuable tool for networking and career development.

Meetup provides a platform for individuals to discover and join local groups centred around shared interests. This can be an excellent avenue for connecting with professionals in the same industry who reside nearby. By fostering in-person interactions, Meetup facilitates stronger professional relationships and potential collaborations.

Industry-specific Platforms

Industry-specific platforms have revolutionized the way professionals connect, collaborate, and learn. These online communities offer a wealth of knowledge, insights, and networking opportunities.

Reddit, a vast online forum, hosts numerous subreddits dedicated to specific industries and professions. By joining relevant subreddits, individuals can participate in discussions, share expertise, and connect with like-minded professionals. This platform fosters a sense of community and allows for the exchange of ideas and experiences.

Quora, another question-and-answer platform, provides a space to ask questions, provide answers, and connect with experts in various fields. This platform empowers individuals to seek guidance, share insights, and learn from the collective wisdom of the community.

In addition to these general platforms, many industries have their own online forums or discussion boards. By participating in these industry-specific communities, professionals can stay updated on the latest trends, connect with peers, and seek advice from experienced individuals.

Online Communities and Events

The professional landscape thrives on connections. In today's digital age, a wealth of online communities and events exist to help individuals build their networks and stay ahead of the curve.

Social media platforms offer a fantastic starting point. Joining Facebook groups specific to your industry fosters discussions, resource sharing, and valuable connections with colleagues. Similarly, following industry influencers and engaging in relevant conversations on Twitter expands your reach and builds your professional brand.

Looking beyond social media, industry conferences and webinars provide unparalleled opportunities for in-depth learning and networking. These events connect you with professionals in your field, expose you to emerging trends, and spark potential collaborations.

For a comprehensive view of upcoming business events, 10times.com is an invaluable resource. This platform curates details on conferences, trade shows, and exhibitions across diverse industries. With a user-friendly search by location, date, and sector, you can easily discover events that align with your professional goals. These events facilitate networking, knowledge acquisition, and potential market exploration, all key elements to success in today's dynamic business environment.

Tips for Effective Networking

Effective networking is a crucial skill for professionals seeking to advance their careers. Online platforms have revolutionized the way we connect with others, making it easier than ever to build and maintain professional relationships.

To maximize the benefits of online networking, it's essential to complete your profile accurately and keep it up-to-date. Actively engaging in discussions, sharing valuable content, and responding to messages can help you build strong relationships. Joining relevant groups and communities allows you to connect with like-minded professionals and stay informed about industry trends. Attending virtual or in-person events provides opportunities to meet people face-to-face and expand your network.

After connecting with someone, it's important to follow up with a personalized message to continue the conversation. By utilizing these online platforms and following these tips, you can effectively network with industry professionals, expand your knowledge, and advance your career.

Beyond online networking, building strong relationships with potential buyers, suppliers, and logistics providers is crucial for successful exporting. A comprehensive business plan outlining your export goals, strategies, and financial projections can help you navigate the complexities of international trade and achieve long-term success.

Gathering Data

Accurate and up-to-date data on both buyers and sellers is essential for success in international trade. While sourcing information on domestic sellers may be relatively straightforward, acquiring validated data on foreign buyers can be more challenging.

Various methods and tools can assist in identifying potential buyers for your export business. However, it's important to note that this list is not exhaustive, and other approaches may be suitable for your specific needs.

Navigating the complexities of international trade requires access to reliable tools and resources. Indian Missions provide targeted assistance for export inquiries, while comprehensive platforms like the India Trade Portal and Export Import Data Bank offer valuable insights. Additionally, tools such as port data analysis and G Maps Extractor can streamline operations, from identifying potential importers to analysing trade flows.

- **Indian Missions**—The Ministry of External Affairs (MEA) maintains an up-to-date list of Indian missions abroad.

    To get contact details of the Indian missions abroad:

    Step 1. Visit MEA website: *https://www.mea.gov.in/indian-mission-abroad.htm.*

    Step 2. Select your target country.

    On the MEA website, choose the country where you'd like to find importers of a specific product. This will display the contact details of the corresponding Indian mission in that country.

    Step 3. Introduce yourself and request information.

    Compose a concise email introducing yourself and your company. Clearly state your request for information on potential importers of the product. Mention the relevant HS code for clarity.

    Refer to *Annexure A* for a sample email format.

NOTE:

- <u>Avoid CC/BCC</u>: When contacting different missions, send separate emails to each one. Avoid using CC or BCC to prevent cluttering their inboxes and expedite responses.
- <u>Response Time</u>: Most missions respond within 3-4 business days.

- **DGFT Portal**—The DGFT Portal is an online platform developed by the Indian government to support exporters and importers. Key features include IEC registration, applying for export-related licenses (e.g., Advance Authorization, EPCG), and accessing export incentive schemes like RoDTEP and MEIS. It allows exporters to track their export obligations, stay updated on trade policies through notifications, and apply for Certificates of Origin for tariff benefits. The portal also offers an online grievance redressal system. The platform enhances convenience, transparency, and cost-efficiency by digitizing processes, reducing paperwork, and ensuring real-time tracking. Overall, it supports India's exporters in complying with trade regulations, accessing government benefits, and staying competitive in global markets.

- **India Trade Portal**—The Indian Trade Portal is a comprehensive online platform designed to facilitate international trade for Indian businesses. Its key functions are to provide trade information, provide expert advice, provide information on India's export-import policies and procedures, and many more.

- **Export Import Data Bank**—The Export Import Data Bank (EIDB) is a valuable resource provided by the Ministry of Commerce and Industry, Government of India. It serves as a repository of detailed information on India's import and export activities.

- **Port Data**—Port Data refers to the collection of information about the activities and operations of a port. This data includes various aspects such as cargo handling, vessel traffic, container movement, revenue generation, and infrastructure development.

Several private companies, including Volza, Trade Genius, Katariya International, Kpler, Panjiva, Descartes Datamyne, ImportYeti, Zauba, and Seair Exim Solutions collect and analyse port data for various purposes. However, it's important to note that these services are typically provided on a subscription basis and may incur costs.

- **Trademap**—Trade Map is a resourceful platform that provides detailed trade statistics to support international business development. It offers insights into export performance, global demand, competitive markets, and trade flows across 220 countries and 5,300 products. You can access data through tables, graphs, and maps, and explore market trends at various levels of detail, from aggregated statistics to specific tariff lines. The platform is valuable for identifying import/export opportunities, market trends, and potential business partners, making it particularly beneficial for businesses looking to enhance their export strategies.

- **Alibaba**—Alibaba is a paid and global e-commerce platform connecting suppliers and buyers worldwide, focusing on B2B trade. It enables businesses to source products in bulk, explore a wide range of industries, and access a global marketplace for import/export opportunities. While you can connect with potential buyers through Alibaba's messaging system and business listings, it is not designed for extracting buyers' data directly. Instead, it facilitates communication and negotiation with interested parties, making it a valuable platform for finding leads and building business relationships.

- **Indiamart**—IndiaMART is an online marketplace connecting buyers and suppliers across India. It allows businesses to list products and services, facilitating B2B transactions. You can use IndiaMART to find potential buyers, explore supplier profiles, and contact them directly. While you can gather buyer data, accessing specific contact details may require a paid membership or subscription, depending on the level of access you need. The platform is useful for identifying buyers, expanding your reach, and enhancing your export business strategies.

- **Trade India**—TradeIndia is an online business-to-business (B2B) marketplace connecting Indian manufacturers, suppliers, and exporters with global buyers. It allows businesses to list their products, showcase their services, and reach potential buyers. You can use TradeIndia to gather buyer data, such as contact information, and explore international trade opportunities. However, access to detailed buyer data often requires registration and may involve paid plans depending on the depth of information you seek. It's an excellent resource for finding buyers and expanding your export business.

Capturing and Storing Data

In the modern era, data serves as the foundation for informed decision-making, strategic planning, and operational efficiency. Capturing and storing data enables organisations to maintain a record of transactions, track progress, and identify trends that inform critical business decisions. Properly stored data ensures accuracy, enhances accountability, and provides a reliable basis for forecasting and analysis. Furthermore, it serves as an invaluable resource for evaluating performance, measuring success, and identifying areas for improvement.

Spreadsheet Applications as Tools for Data Storage

Spreadsheet applications such as Google Sheets and Microsoft Excel are widely regarded as essential tools for storing and managing data. These applications provide a flexible, user-friendly interface that accommodates a wide range of data types, from numerical values and text entries to dates and formulas. Their powerful functionalities, such as filtering, sorting, and conditional formatting, allow users to organise and visualise data effectively. Additionally, their ability to handle large datasets makes them suitable for both personal and professional use.

Google Sheets offers the added advantage of cloud-based accessibility, enabling real-time collaboration and seamless sharing among team members. Microsoft Excel, renowned for its robust analytical tools and advanced features such as PivotTables and macros, remains a preferred choice for complex data manipulation. Both platforms support integrations with other software, making them highly versatile for various data-driven applications.

By capturing data in well-structured formats and utilising tools like comments or notes, organisations can not only preserve information but also enrich it with insights that improve clarity and usability. These practices ultimately enhance data's role as a cornerstone of effective decision-making.

Tools and Resources

In today's export business, software applications are pivotal in improving efficiency, minimising errors, and streamlining operations. These tools assist with documentation, shipment tracking, tariff calculation, and regulatory compliance. By automating routine tasks, software solutions free up time for strategic decision-making, increase productivity, and help exporters maintain competitiveness.

Certain software applications are essential for enhancing productivity in the export business. While some are available for free, others may require payment. This list is not exhaustive, and you may choose to explore additional tools based on your specific needs.

- **Wabulk.net**—The Wabulk.net provides a set of tools and extensions designed to enhance WhatsApp usage, particularly for business and privacy purposes. Its key features include the ability to export WhatsApp contacts in various formats (CSV, Excel, JSON), filter and verify WhatsApp numbers for targeted messaging campaigns, and a privacy extension that secures WhatsApp Web by hiding sensitive information with blur effects. These tools help users manage contacts, ensure campaign efficiency, and maintain privacy while using WhatsApp for communication.

- **Email Extractor**—The Email Extractor extension for Chrome is a tool designed to help users collect email addresses from websites, social media platforms, or online directories. It automatically scans web pages and extracts email addresses, making it easier for marketers, business owners, or anyone needing to build an email list. The extension simplifies the process by saving time and effort, especially for bulk email extraction. However, it's important to use this tool responsibly to comply with privacy regulations and avoid spamming.

- **Bulk Email Senders**—The Bulk email sender programs are software tools that allow businesses or individuals to send large volumes of emails at once, often for marketing campaigns, newsletters, or notifications.

Bulk email sending is a powerful and cost-effective marketing tool, allowing you to reach a global audience efficiently. Its strengths lie in its ability to deliver personalized and targeted messages, track performance metrics, and integrate seamlessly with other marketing platforms. However, it also faces challenges like spam filters, low open rates, and potential deliverability issues. To succeed, you must navigate these weaknesses by focusing on quality content, proper list management, and robust authentication protocols like SPF and DKIM.

Compliance with regulations such as GDPR and CAN-SPAM is crucial to avoid legal repercussions and maintain customer trust. Additionally, while email campaigns offer significant opportunities for brand building and customer engagement, they are threatened by phishing risks, reputation damage, and over-reliance on third-party tools. Risk mitigation strategies include adhering to legal frameworks, maintaining up-to-date recipient lists, and using reputable email platforms to enhance deliverability and security.

Ultimately, the success of bulk email campaigns hinges on providing valuable, engaging, and relevant content to the right audience. By leveraging advanced analytics, segmentation, and automation, businesses can maximize the potential of email marketing while mitigating the risks of non-compliance, technical issues, and customer dissatisfaction.

Here are 5 popular bulk email senders:

- <u>Mailchimp</u>—Offers email marketing automation, templates, and analytics for creating and sending bulk emails efficiently.

- <u>Brevo</u>—Provides email campaigns, SMS, and marketing automation tools for bulk email distribution.

- <u>Benchmark Email</u>—Focuses on email marketing with an intuitive interface, automation, and analytics features.

- <u>Moosend</u>—Delivers powerful email marketing tools, including automation and list management, ideal for bulk email campaigns.

- AWeber—Known for email automation, segmentation, and analytics, AWeber helps businesses send bulk emails effectively.

- **Bulk Whatsapp Sender**—Bulk WhatsApp sender programs are tools used to send messages to large numbers of recipients simultaneously, ideal for marketing, notifications, or customer outreach. They allow businesses to reach wide audiences efficiently.

  Bulk WhatsApp sending offers strengths like cost-efficiency, wide reach, and direct customer engagement. Its weaknesses include risks of spam, limited message customization, and potential account bans. Opportunities lie in personalized marketing and enhanced brand visibility. Threats include regulatory scrutiny, legal penalties, and data privacy concerns. To mitigate risks, businesses should comply with WhatsApp policies, use authorized APIs, focus on value-driven messaging, and ensure customer consent to avoid spam and maintain trust.

  To send bulk WhatsApp messages through authorized channels, businesses should utilize the WhatsApp Business API provided by official Business Solution Providers (BSPs). These BSPs are approved by WhatsApp to offer API access and additional services, ensuring compliance with WhatsApp's policies and maintaining high message deliverability.

  Here are some notable authorized BSPs:

  - Twilio—Twilio offers robust APIs for WhatsApp messaging, enabling businesses to engage customers personally and integrate WhatsApp into their communication strategies.

  - Bird—Bird provides a comprehensive platform for WhatsApp Business API, facilitating seamless customer interactions across various channels.

  - Wati—Wati specializes in offering WhatsApp API solutions tailored for businesses, enhancing customer engagement through efficient messaging tools.

- <u>360dialog</u>—360dialog is known for its straightforward integration process, providing businesses with direct access to WhatsApp Business API for effective communication.

- <u>Clickatell</u>—Clickatell, a global Meta Business Partner, offers advanced messaging solutions and payments integration via the WhatsApp Business API.

To find a comprehensive list of authorized BSPs, refer to the Meta Partner Directory.

Key Considerations When Choosing a BSP

- <u>Compliance</u>—Ensure the provider strictly adheres to WhatsApp's terms of service to prevent account bans.

- <u>Scalability</u>—Select a BSP that can handle your current and anticipated message volumes.

- <u>Integration</u>—Look for providers that offer seamless integration with your existing CRM and other business tools.

- <u>Support</u>—Opt for BSPs that provide robust customer support to assist with technical and operational queries.

By partnering with an authorized BSP, you can effectively send bulk WhatsApp messages while ensuring compliance and maintaining high-quality customer interactions.

- **Instant Messaging Applications**—Instant messaging applications allow users to send real-time text messages, voice notes, and multimedia. They enable instant communication, group chats, and voice/video calls, making them essential for both personal and professional use.

  The popular instant messaging apps are *WhatsApp*, *Viber*, *Botim*, *Skype* and *Telegram*.

- **10times.com**—10times.com is a global event discovery platform that lists trade shows, exhibitions, conferences, and business events across various industries. It helps exporters find relevant events to network, showcase products, and explore new markets. By attending these events, exporters can connect with potential buyers, suppliers, and partners, boosting their visibility and expanding their international reach. The platform offers details on event schedules, locations, and registration, making it a valuable tool for businesses aiming to stay competitive and informed.

- **G Maps Extractor**—G Maps Extractor provides a tool for extracting business data from Google Maps. It gathers information such as business names, phone numbers, emails, social media profiles, addresses, websites, reviews, ratings, and more. The data can be exported in formats like CSV, JSON, or Excel for use in lead generation or analysis. It offers free and paid plans.

- **Apollo.io**—Apollo.io is a comprehensive platform designed to facilitate the identification of detailed contact information for professionals, including prominent individuals across various industries. It offers access to email addresses, phone numbers, and LinkedIn profiles, aiding users in lead generation and sales outreach efforts. The platform leverages a proprietary database and publicly accessible information to deliver precise data. It is worth noting that certain advanced features or detailed records may require a paid subscription.

Conclusion

As we conclude this comprehensive journey through the world of exporting, it becomes clear that success in international trade is not merely about selling products across borders—it is about vision, strategy, and resilience. "Unlocking Global Markets" encapsulates the essence of what it takes to thrive in the dynamic global marketplace.

Through meticulous planning, robust execution, and leveraging India's unique strengths, exporters can transform challenges into opportunities. The insights shared on navigating regulations, understanding market dynamics, and embracing innovation lay a solid foundation for sustainable growth. Moreover, the book underscores the pivotal role of collaboration—with government bodies, export promotion councils, and logistics partners—showcasing how these alliances can amplify success.

Exporting is as much about creating value as it is about building relationships and trust in global markets. By embracing the principles and strategies outlined in this book, Indian exporters can position themselves as not just participants but leaders in international trade. With a thriving export ecosystem and unyielding entrepreneurial spirit, India is poised to continue its ascent as a global powerhouse. This book invites every reader to be a part of this transformative journey, to take bold steps, and to unlock their potential in the world of global commerce.

Annexure A: Sample Email Format

Subject: Inquiry – [Product Name] Importers in [Country Name]

Dear Sir/Madam,

My name is [Your Name] and I represent [Your Company Name], a company specializing in [Product Name].

We are interested in exploring opportunities to export our products to [Country Name]. Could you please provide us with information on potential importers of [Product Name] (HS code: NNNNNNNN) in your region?

Thank you for your time and assistance.

Sincerely,

[Your Name]
[Designation], [Your Company Name]

Annexure B: Sample Joint Venture / Memorandum of Understanding Document

JOINT VENTURE AGREEMENT

(FOR EXPORTING PRODUCTS GLOBALLY)

This Joint Venture Agreement ("Agreement") is entered into on this ___ day of ________, [year] (the "Effective Date"), by and between:

1. **[SELLER NAME]**, a sole proprietorship/private limited company, having GSTIN [_________] and its registered office at [ADDRESS] (hereinafter referred to as the "Seller" or "First Party"); and

2. **[INTRODUCER NAME]**, an individual having PAN [________] and residing at [ADDRESS] (hereinafter referred to as the "Introducer" or "Second Party"),

(Hereinafter collectively referred to as the "Parties" and individually as a "Party").

WHEREAS:

A. The Seller is engaged in the business of manufacturing and selling goods (the "Products").

B. The Introducer has established contacts and relationships with prospective buyers located outside India and is desirous of introducing such buyers to the Seller for the purpose of promoting the export of the Seller's Products.

C. The Parties wish to collaborate to facilitate the export of the Seller's Products to international markets on the terms and conditions set forth herein.

NOW, THEREFORE, in consideration of the mutual promises and covenants contained herein, the Parties agree as follows:

1. APPOINTMENT

1.1. The Seller hereby appoints the Introducer as an intermediary to identify and introduce prospective international buyers ("Buyers") to the Seller for the export of the Products.

1.2. This Agreement explicitly limits the Introducer's role to the global export market. The Introducer shall have no authority, rights, or involvement in the Seller's domestic market operations or sales within India.

1.3. The Introducer shall act in good faith and in compliance with applicable laws to introduce Buyers not already known to the Seller and to promote the export of the Products globally.

1.4. The Parties agree that this Agreement governs all transactions and defines the rights and liabilities of the Parties. No additional documents shall override the terms herein unless mutually agreed upon in writing.

2. TERM AND TERMINATION

2.1. This Agreement shall commence on the Effective Date and remain in effect until terminated by either Party by providing _____________ [number of days] days' written notice to the other Party.

2.2. Upon termination, the Parties shall complete any pending obligations, including payment of fees due to the Introducer.

3. RIGHTS AND OBLIGATIONS OF THE PARTIES

3.1. Obligations of the Seller

    a. The Seller shall provide the Introducer with up-to-date product information, catalogues, pricing, and promotional materials to enable the Introducer to promote the Products.

b.   The Seller shall ensure the timely delivery of Products to Buyers and provide all export documentation necessary for customs clearance and compliance with applicable laws.

c.   The Seller shall remain responsible for obtaining and maintaining all certifications, licenses, and government approvals required for the export of the Products.

d.   The Seller shall communicate directly with the Buyers introduced by the Introducer and ensure that payments for export transactions are received in accordance with the agreed terms.

e.   The Seller shall not involve the Introducer in any domestic sales or transactions within India.

3.2. Obligations of the Introducer

a.   The Introducer shall identify and introduce potential Buyers located outside India to the Seller and assist in facilitating export transactions.

b.   The Introducer shall disclose all relevant details of Buyers to the Seller and act solely as an introducer, without binding the Seller in any financial or contractual arrangements.

c.   The Introducer shall not claim or exercise any authority over the Seller's domestic operations or marketing efforts.

d.   The Introducer shall ensure compliance with all applicable laws, including export regulations and anti-corruption laws, while performing its obligations under this Agreement.

4. COMMISSION AND PAYMENT TERMS

4.1. All sales facilitated or effected by the Introducer, which directly result in the Seller's revenue generation, shall entitle the Introducer to a commission from the Seller. The terms and conditions governing the commission shall be as set forth hereunder:

   a. For the initial order placed by a specific Buyer for a specific Product, the Seller hereby covenants to pay the Introducer a commission equivalent to fifty percent (50%) of the net profit derived from such export transactions directly attributable to the efforts of the Introducer.

   b. For any subsequent orders of the same Product from the same Buyer, the Seller agrees to remunerate the Introducer with a commission amounting to thirty percent (30%) of the net profit accrued from such transactions.

   c. The term "net profit" shall be construed as the gross revenue realized from the transaction, less all associated costs, including but not limited to production expenses, logistics costs, and applicable taxes.

   d. In the event that the existing Buyer places an order for Products different from those already supplied, the Seller agrees to pay the Introducer a commission equivalent to fifty percent (50%) of the net profit generated from such export transactions, provided that such transactions result directly from the efforts of the Introducer.

4.2. The commission shall be paid within seven (7) calendar days of the Seller receiving payment from the Buyer. The Introducer shall issue an invoice for the commission, and payment shall be made via bank transfer.

4.3. The Seller shall not be obligated to pay commission for domestic transactions or export transactions conducted independently of the Introducer.

5. CONFIDENTIALITY

5.1. Each Party agrees to keep all confidential information received from the other Party secure and not to disclose such information to any third party without prior written consent, except as required by law.

5.2. Confidential information includes, but is not limited to, Buyer details, pricing, trade secrets, and any other sensitive business information.

5.3. Upon termination of this Agreement, all confidential information shall be returned to the disclosing Party or destroyed upon written request.

6. NON-COMPETE

6.1. During the term of this Agreement and for six (6) months thereafter, the Seller shall not directly or indirectly:

    a. Solicit Buyers introduced by the Introducer to conduct business outside the scope of this Agreement; or

    b. Engage in any activities that would circumvent the Introducer's role as specified herein.

7. WARRANTIES AND INDEMNITY

7.1. Both Parties represent and warrant that they have the authority to enter into this Agreement and that their respective obligations will be performed in compliance with applicable laws.

7.2. Each Party agrees to indemnify and hold harmless the
other Party against any losses, damages, or penalties
arising from breaches of this Agreement or violations of
applicable laws.

8. GOVERNING LAW AND DISPUTE RESOLUTION

8.1. This Agreement shall be governed by and construed in
accordance with the laws of India. The courts of
[SPECIFY JURISDICTION] shall have exclusive
jurisdiction over any disputes arising under this
Agreement.

8.2. 8.2 Any dispute or difference arising out of or in
connection with this Agreement shall be resolved by
arbitration in accordance with the Arbitration and
Conciliation Act, 1996. The arbitration shall be
conducted in English, and the seat of arbitration shall be
[SPECIFY LOCATION].

9. ENTIRE AGREEMENT

This Agreement constitutes the entire understanding between the
Parties concerning its subject matter and supersedes all prior
agreements, understandings, or representations.

10. AMENDMENTS

No amendment or modification of this Agreement shall be valid
unless made in writing and signed by both Parties.

SIGNATURES

IN WITNESS WHEREOF, the Parties hereto have executed this
Agreement as of the Effective Date.

For the Seller:

Name: _______________________________

Signature: _______________________________

Date: _______________________________

For the Introducer:

Name: _______________________________

Signature: _______________________________

Date: _______________________________

Witness 1:

Name: _______________________________

Signature: _______________________________

Witness 2:

Name: _______________________________

Signature: _______________________________